Contents

		Page
1	Childhood	1
2	The Young Star	6
3	Film Superstar	11
4	Ups and Downs	19

1 Childhood

She is one of the highest paid actresses
in Hollywood.
She is married to Bruce Willis,
a famous actor.
She is beautiful.

She seems to have everything.
But life has not always been kind
to Demi Moore.

Before Demi was even born
her father left home.

She was born in New Mexico
on 11 November 1962.
She was given the name Demetria.

Demi grew up thinking
that her stepfather, Danny,
was her real father.

Danny kept changing jobs.
The family moved house
at least twice a year.

So Demi and her little brother
had a hard time making friends.

Demi was 15 years old
when she found out
who her real father was.

She was a lonely girl
who had a lazy eye.
She had to wear an eye patch
and she had two eye operations
to cure it.

Demi's parents were not happy.
They kept on drinking and fighting
until one day her stepfather
killed himself.

After Danny's death
the family moved to LA
to make a new start.

They lived in a block of flats
next door to an actress.
Demi often helped the actress
to learn her lines.

Demi said to herself:
'This is what I want to do.'
She saw acting as a way out and up.

So when Demi was 16
she left school and home
to try and get into acting.

At first she got work
posing for pin-up photos.

When she was 18
she married Freddy Moore.
He was a British rock musician.

They divorced after four years.
Some years later Demi found out
that he was already married
when he married her.

2 The Young Star

Also at 18 years old,
Demi got her first regular work.
She beat a thousand others
for a part in the TV drama
General Hospital.

Now she was on TV every week.
This sudden burst of fame
was very hard for Demi to cope with.

She started drinking too much
and taking drugs.
She was too young to cope.
She said:
'I had no idea of who I was
or what my ideas were.'

The young Demi Moore.

Demi had a few small parts in films
while she worked in TV.
In one film
she was chased by giant slugs!

She had to work
on *General Hospital* for two years
until her big break came.

She left the TV drama
for a part in the film *St Elmo's Fire*,
about a group of friends.
For a few years the same young actors
always seemed to be
making films together.
Demi was part of that group.

But one day she turned up for work
high on drugs.
Everyone saw her.

Demi was very nearly fired.
She put herself into a clinic
to come off drugs.
When she was well again,
she asked to go back to work.

They let her finish the film
and it was a big hit.
It was a hard lesson
and she has stayed off drugs
ever since.

Many years later,
Demi put her mother
into the same clinic
but it did not work for her.

Demi did not see her mother
for a long time after that.
Lately they have met again
but sadly her mother is very ill.

Demi Moore with Bruce Willis.

3 Film Superstar

In 1987 she met Bruce Willis.
He was the star of a TV comedy drama.
In many ways
they were made for each other.
They both had hard lives.

Three months later they got married.
Rock superstar Little Richard
sang at their wedding.

A year later
their first daughter was born.

At that time Demi's film career
seemed to be cursed
like the other young actors she had worked with.
Some of them
have never worked again since those days.

But in 1990
her new film *Ghost*
opened at cinemas.
It was the year's biggest hit
and it was a real tear-jerker.

Suddenly Demi Moore
was a film superstar.

In 1991 Demi's films flopped.
But she had made sure
that she was still a star.
She did this by using her talent
for publicity.

She agreed to be on the cover
of a magazine called *Vanity Fair*.
She was naked
and seven months pregnant.
It proved that women can be
pregnant and sexy.

Her second daughter was born
later that year.

The next year she was back
on the cover of *Vanity Fair*.
Again she was naked
but this time
she was covered in body paint.

Demi had another box office hit
in 1992 with Tom Cruise.
It was called *A Few Good Men*.

Then she was in
a string of films
that got people talking.

In 1994
Demi got people talking
with the film *Disclosure*.

She played the part
of a ruthless woman
who harasses a man at work.

Her third daughter
was born in the same year.

Demi and Bruce have chosen
to bring up their three girls
on a ranch in Idaho.
It's one of their three homes.

With Bruce and two of their daughters.

In 1996
Demi was paid a lot of money
to be a model again.

In 1996 Demi was also chosen
as one of the 50
most beautiful people in the world.

Then she was asked to
play the part of a stripper
in the film *Striptease*.

Demi was paid $12 million
for her part in this film.
In that year
she was the highest paid actress
in the world.

Now she was paid as much
as the men in films.

4 Ups and Downs

To advertise *Striptease*
Demi stripped off
on a TV chat show.

Everyone saw the good shape
her body was in.
Some said
she'd had plastic surgery.
Others said it was down to training at the gym.

Demi used the same ploy
to advertise her 1997 film *GI Jane*.
She went on the same chat show
but this time
with her head shaved.
She did one arm push ups.

Demi played a soldier in *GI Jane*.

Demi had to get super fit
for her part in *GI Jane*.
She did all her own stunts.

She plays a soldier
who is chosen
for Navy Seal training.
They want to see if women
are fit for combat.

Sadly the film was not a big hit.
Some people said
it was so bad
that they gave Demi
a joke award for worst actress.

It seems that
Demi's success rate in films
goes up and down like a yoyo.
But her career does not.

She is very clever
when she advertises herself.

Demi doesn't talk
to the newspapers very often.
She feels they don't like her success.

But we still see photos of her
everywhere.

We see photos of Demi everywhere.

Demi Moore's critics say
she's just one more beautiful body
and she can't act.

But her films make billions of dollars
at the box office.

In 1997 alone she made four films.
She works very hard indeed.

But she doesn't just act.
Demi is also a very successful
businesswoman.

Bruce and Demi
have put money into a burger chain
called Planet Hollywood.

She uses her talent for publicity
to make it a success.

They turn up every time
a new Planet Hollywood opens.
The 28th one opened in LA in 1998.

With Arnold Schwarzenegger and 'Sly' Stallone at Planet Hollywood, LA.

Today Demi Moore is a powerful woman
in Hollywood.

But her life is changing.
Demi and Bruce
have said they are splitting up.

Maybe they spent too much time apart.

They have millions of dollars
to share out
and children to think of.

She will need all her talent
to re-make herself.
But she is a strong woman.
She has come too far to give up now.